Encouragement
for the
Discouraged

A YOUNG GIRL'S INVITATION TO COURAGE THROUGH DYSLEXIA

Includes creative ideas, uplifting scriptures,
and bonus notes for parents.

Abigail Winslow

ISBN: 978-1-7165-0555-3 (sc)
ISBN: 978-1-7165-0553-9 (e)

Lulu Publishing Services rev. date: 10/20/2020

Dedication

This book is dedicated to Ms. Diane Draper, my Barton Reading Specialist, who is helping me learn how to read, spell and write.

Epigraph

"I can do all things through Christ who strengthens me."
Philippians 4:13 NKJV

TABLE OF CONTENTS

FOREWORD

Abby has been called the "never give up girl"
since she was old enough to walk. She has shown
a passion for overcoming obstacles both big and
small. I'm so grateful for how she shares that
passion and courage on the pages of this book.

She is a gift to us, and I know her heart will
be a gift to you as well. Many blessings of
grace and peace on your hearts and home.

Francie (Abby's mom)

PREFACE

I wrote this book after I found out that I had dyslexia
and dysgraphia. Dyslexia is a reading challenge, and
dysgraphia is a writing challenge. These challenges
made school hard and made me feel really discouraged.
I felt like I was alone in it because not a lot of people
I know have these challenges. School was really hard,
and many days I felt really sad and overwhelmed.

I didn't want other kids who have challenges
like mine to feel as discouraged as I did.

That's where I got the idea to write this book.
Plus, I really like to encourage people.

ACKNOWLEDGMENT

I would like to thank my mom and my dad who encouraged me to complete this book. Thank you, Dad, for helping me believe I could do it. Thank you mom for typing while I dictated this book.

INTRODUCTION

In this book, you will get encouragement,
inspiration and some new ideas that will help
you remember that God cares for you, and that
you were made to overcome hard challenges.

In the back, parents will find an extra bit of
encouragement, with practical ideas on how to love
and encourage their kids through hard times.

CHAPTER 1

DISCOURAGEMENT HURTS

*T*HIS YEAR AT the dinner table, my dad started talking about the philosophy of freedom. That sounds a little confusing, right? But it's really all about how powerful our choices are. And that we are free to make powerful choices everyday.

During those chats, I realized that I had been feeling discouraged without having the words to describe it. So I started *choosing* to tell my mom and dad that I felt discouraged, a lot.

Being discouraged can sometimes feel like no one wants you and no one believes that you can do anything. It can make your heart feel sad and lonely. Feeling discouraged means that your heart hurts because people may have hurt your feelings or because you feel like you don't fit in. Or maybe something is harder for you than for others.

For me, fitting in is hard because I can't do things like other people. I have a hard time with school. So here's what I think you can do if you are feeling discouraged too.

I suggest that you start telling your parents and family when you feel discouraged.

You can say, "Something/someone has hurt my feelings today and I'm feeling a little discouraged."

Just talking about it helps you feel better. And talking about it reminds you that you are not alone.

REMEMBER:
YOU ARE NOT ALONE

If school is really hard, you can ask your mom or dad to help you find out if you have dyslexia or dysgraphia, or some other learning challenge. I have dyslexia and dysgraphia so school has been difficult for me. Having dyslexia is something that makes you struggle with more reading problems than most kids. Dysgraphia is a challenge that makes writing difficult.

These learning challenges can feel very overwhelming and discouraging. Many days, when it's time for school, I get overwhelmed and feel like everything will be too hard. In those times, I feel discouraged. But I am learning to remind myself that I am not alone.

You Matter To God Scripture:

"Be strong and courageous. Do not be afraid or terrified because of them, for the LORD your God goes with you; he will never leave you nor forsake you." Deuteronomy 31:6 NIV

CHAPTER 2

GROWTH MINDSET

O NE OF MY favorite parts of school this year was learning about something called "Growth Mindset". I highly suggest you learn about growth mindset, too. There's a big difference between a fixed mindset and a growth mindset.

A fixed mindset is when you say "I cannot do this!" Or "that person does things way better than me." Or "I quit!" That's called comparison and comparing yourself to others just adds to the discouragement.

A growth mindset is when you say "I *can* do this!" Or "If I keep practicing, I *know* I can get better!"

Even when you fail, remember to tell yourself "It's okay! I'm failing forward!"

Some other growth mindset statements
for your hard days could be:

- I am an overcomer.
- If I struggle, I can ask for help.
- This is hard, but that doesn't mean I can't do it.
- I will keep trying until it gets easier.
- I am learner.
- I am growing, I will get better.
- I can't do this very well, *YET.*

Knowing about a growth mindset has helped me feel better because it helps me overcome negative thoughts and keep moving forward.

You Matter to God Scripture:

"I can do all things through Christ who strengthens me." Philippians 4:13

CHAPTER 3

KNOW YOU ARE
NOT ALONE

I F YOU FEEL sad, know that you are not alone. God is with you and so are the adults who love you. When I get discouraged, sometimes I feel weak and lonely. But I have to remember I am NEVER alone.

If you feel sad or alone, one suggestion is to find help to do whatever it is you're trying to do. For example, if you got a bracelet making kit, and you don't know how to do it, you should say, "Can I have some help please?"

If school is hard, you can ask your teacher or parent for extra help. For me, I'm homeschooled and that helps my dyslexia because I have my mom and dad close by. I also have a tutor who is helping me learn how to read. You should never feel scared of getting a tutor or asking for help.

I have also learned that I never have to keep my feelings inside and to myself. Sharing my feelings with the people in my life who care for me, and sharing my feelings with God has been really helpful.

When I share my feelings with those who love me, it strengthens me. And everytime I share my feelings, I get stronger and less afraid to talk about how I am really doing. The more I share, the less I feel afraid and alone.

You matter to God Scripture:

> "So be strong and courageous! Do not be afraid and do not panic before them. For the LORD your God will personally go ahead of you. **He will neither fail you nor abandon you.**" (Deuteronomy 31:6 NLT)

CHAPTER 4

THE POWER OF ART

B EING CREATIVE CAN help you relax and find your way through discouraging moments. For me, I *love* doing art. It makes me calm down and feel more peaceful. Finding the right colors when I am painting a beautiful picture on a canvas really helps me feel better.

My grandma gave me some acrylic paint when I was younger. I've always had them in my art space. When I am discouraged I go to my art space, pick out a fresh canvas, put it on an easel and then I just paint what I feel.

Sometimes I see an amazing sight on a road trip or at the beach and I try to paint that. I like painting things when I feel sad. I like to do an ocean picture of a beach to help me feel like I am getting washed clean by the waves. When I see God's colorful creativity I feel refreshed and hopeful.

I also like painting something called a Feelings Chart. A Feelings Chart helps me explain what I feel. I use colors to represent feelings. On my Feelings Chart, the cooler colors (like blue and green) represent sad and discouraged. The warmer colors (like pink and red) represent my feelings of joy, happiness and love. And I have a purple stroke that goes down the side of all the colors to remind myself that God feels all of those things with me.

I really like my Feelings Chart. I would recommend making your own and framing it or putting it on a wall where you can see it at all times. My Feelings Chart helps me identify how I feel, and once I know how am feeling, I can tell my parents more about how I am doing. I think a Feelings Chart may help you too.

Remember:

God feels everything WITH you. He is there for you.

You Matter to God Scripture:

"In the beginning, God created the heavens and the earth. And it was good."
Genesis 1:1 ESV

CHAPTER 5

EXERCISE IS GOOD!

A NOTHER IDEA FOR overcoming discouragement is to exercise. Exercise gets the blood flowing inside your body. That makes you feel more happy and joyful. It often helps my mom and dad, too.

One day when I was feeling low, my mom told me to try and move my body. I made a list of all the workouts I knew how to do. These were burpees, pushups, pull-ups and jumping jacks. When I spent time doing the exercises on my list, I noticed that I was feeling happier and more joyful.

God made our bodies powerful because when we use them well, it brings us more feelings of energy and happiness.

You matter to God Scripture:

"For you formed my inward parts; you knitted me together in my mother's womb. I praise you, for I am fearfully and wonderfully made. Wonderful are your works; my soul knows it very well." Psalm 139:13-14 ESV

CHAPTER 6

WHY I LOVE CHURCH

WHEN I GO to church, I feel happy and joyful. The worship reminds me of how God loves us. We have a lot of friends there and specifically, there is a really nice lady who usually brings us toys and books to look at. At church, we learn about Jesus and become more hopeful. Everytime I go to church, I get more and more belief in God. He is very good to me and I love him with all my heart. I think you can go to church if you don't already.

Church also helps you build strong relationships. And at some churches, they teach you how to pray! I recommend practicing prayer at home too, praying to God for anything you need.

You matter to God Scripture:

"For wherever two or three come together in honor of my name, I am right there with them!" Matthew 18:20 TPT

CHAPTER 7

PRAYER IS EASY AND POWERFUL

THE THING THAT helps me the most in my discouragement is praying to my Lord Jesus. Praying to God will makes me feel less discouraged. Praying helps me feel that God's love is near me. Prayer makes me feel better, even about my dyslexia.

A prayer can sound something like this: "Dear God, thank you for listening to my prayers. I hope you will take care of all of my problems. Help me not feel discouraged. Dear Jesus, I know you will answer my prayers. In Jesus' name, amen."

If you have a different need than me, you can change your prayer. What you say doesn't matter- what matters is that you are telling God about your feelings and letting Him help you.

God loves to know about your feelings and to hear about what happens to you. Knowing this about God makes me feel less alone. And it is comforting to know that someone so powerful loves to listen to my needs and prayers. He is powerful and able to fix things in our lives. Even if there is hard stuff from the past, he can help make it better in the future. My dad struggles with sleep and he has needed to get several doctor appointments to see if he was getting better. But we started praying for him. And I think our prayers for him are working.

When you want to pray, just say

"Jesus I need help. I feel a bit discouraged. Can you please help me?"

Jesus feels good that you are telling him about your needs because he loves you.

You matter to God Scripture:

> **"Don't be pulled in different directions or worried about a thing. Be saturated in prayer throughout each day, offering your**

faith-filled requests before God with overflowing gratitude. Tell him every detail of your life, then God's wonderful peace that transcends human understanding, *will make the answers known to you* through Jesus Christ." Philippians 4:6-8 TPT

CHAPTER 8

DISCOVER INSPIRING PEOPLE

MEET HELEN AND ANNIE

WHEN HELEN KELLER was one, she was a happy baby. She loved to chase rays of sunlight through the house. But what she loved most was to sit in her father's lap and her mother's arms. She felt their comfort and love. But when she turned one, she got struck with a sickness. Finally, when the sickness left her, she could not see or hear.

Then, Ms. Annie came into their lives and said she could help. Ms. Annie used to be blind, too. But after several helpful operations, she could see better, even though her eyes were still weak.

Annie was a patient, creative and kind teacher. One way

she taught Helen about the world was by placing a toy in Helen's hand. On the other hand, Annie would spell the name of that toy with her fingers. She did this with many objects and things so that Helen could enventually "see" with her hands. After many years of working to overcome her challenges and discouragement, Helen grew up, and was able to write and read and speak.

Helen's story is amazing to me. It deeply encouraged me the first time I heard it and still inspires me today. It inspired me to read more books about amazing people who overcame serious discouragement.

Hearing Helen and Annie's story really lifted discouragement off me, as if a heavy sack was lifted from my body. I think that was because her story gave me hope that maybe I can overcome challenges like she did, and be like her when I grow up.

I admire her bravery, and how she overcame her dark, silent world. I am sure it felt very hard for her. But in the end, she became a famous writer whose life inspired people. I hope to be someone who inspires people too.

Jesus loves to help you whenever you need anything! I know this because I have tried praying and when I pray

God fills my heart with his love and his comfort. I know he will love me all the way through.

God thinks you're a blessing and I know he will love you all the way through

You matter to God Scripture:

> "For I know the plans I have for you," declares the Lord, "plans to prosper you and not to harm you, plans to give you hope and a future." Jeremiah 29:11

NOTES FOR PARENTS

WHAT DISCOURAGEMENT FEELS LIKE TO KIDS

Discouragement is real for children. Especially kids with dyslexia or some other challenge.

Feeling discouraged can sometimes feel like no one wants you and no one believes that you can do anything. It can make your heart feel sad and lonely. I have dyslexia and dysgraphia. That makes me feel discouraged. I suggest looking on the internet to learn more about dyslexia to find out if your child has dyslexia or dysgraphia. Dyslexia and dysgraphia are learning differences that can make you feel discouraged and like you don't fit in. Finding that out helps you know what they are going through. If they do have dyslexia or dysgraphia, you can get them a reading tutor that can help them learn in a special way. Learning in new ways can help with the discouragement.

I think a lot of kids feel discouraged, but they don't know how to tell you about it. I would like to share with you some ideas that could help.

1. COMFORT

When your child feels discouraged, you should give them a big hug and comfort them. Parents words are very powerful gifts to comfort discouraged children. You can say loving words like, "I love you, and I am really sorry you're feeling this way." Or "I believe in you." You can even help them through any conflict they are having and by doing this, it makes them feel like you are supporting them and standing up for them. Basically, it makes them feel not alone.

2. TIME SPEAKS LOVE

Spending special time with your kids helps them feel valued and loved. My dad takes each of us kids on a date every Sunday morning. I really like when my dad takes me to a donut place near our house. When we are there, I eat my donut and we talk about my emotions. My dad asks me how I am doing emotionally, and he asks me if I felt discouraged in any way. Then if I did, I can tell him all about my discouragement and what that discouragement felt like. After we talk, I feel more loved than ever and sometimes it even inspires me to write another book, like this one! One day when I was eating my donut with my dad, I had the idea to write this book!

3. NOT ALONE

If your child feels sad, tell them that they are not alone-that God is with them and that you are with them. If they get discouraged sometimes kids feel weak and lonely. You should remind them that they are NEVER alone, and that they never have to keep their feelings inside and to themselves. Keep reminding them that you are always there for them and so is God.

4. PRAYER

You should also encourage your kids to start praying to Jesus and God. Pray with them to show them how easy it is. And be sure to pray for them, when you are with them, and in your own prayer time.

5. ART

You can make a Feelings Chart with your kids. I really think a Feelings Chart can help you connect with how your kids are feeling, too.

Speaking of art, give your kids an art space that is theirs. I would suggest doing arts and crafts with your children. People with dyslexia or other learning challenges are often very good at doing creative things like crafts and I am sure you will find ways that creativity can help with your discouragement. You can also hire a creativity tutor who can help them enjoy art.

6. FEELINGS MATTER

Children's feelings matter. You should tell them to talk about their feelings more often. It makes them feel loved and encouraged.

7. FIND PEOPLE TO HELP

I often feel lonely because I am the only girl in my whole family who has dyslexia. My brother and dad have dyslexia but I am the only girl, and the only one who has dysgraphia. It has felt lonely being the only girl with these learning challenges. But thankfully my parents have found a good reading tutor for me. She helps me alot. She is nice and beautiful. Her name is Ms. Diane. I highly suggest looking her up on the internet. She is a Barton Reading Specialist. Maybe there is someone who can help your child's unique challenges and discouragement. Like a reading or math specialists, or a special counselor or coach.

8. DONUTS ARE GOOD

I suggest all moms or dads start taking their kids to a donut place, or somewhere they can get a cookie or a smoothie. Having something in my belly helps me as I talk about my feelings, especially something yummy. My dad has a special journal. He usually writes my name at the top of the page, then he uses it to fill in all my feelings and goals as we talk. There's a philosopher of freedom named Zig Ziglar. The Ziglar company is the company where my dad got that journal. All parents, I suggest you look for this journal. When he writes my feelings and goals down I feel loved and secure. Because it feels like my dad loves me and knows me. Spending fun time with your kids helps them feel like they are loved.

Please look for more of my books to come. I highly suggest you try looking for them because I feel like my books are pretty good. They can be found in little neighborhood libraries at the top of hills, at parks, in neighborhoods. I try to put my books in those places. I'll let you go, because I know you don't have a lot of time.

BIBLIOGRAPHY

The Performance Planner by Zig Ziglar

Helen Keller: Courage In the Dark by Johanna Hurwitz

Growth Mindset Kit found at BigLifeJournal.com

Here I am with a copy of the Feeling Chart I created. Each color each
represents feelings, and the one purple stripe down the side is there
to remind me that God feels all my feelings, with me. I am NEVER
alone in what I am facing. Making this chart and keeping it nearby
has helped me keep track of and share my feelings more easily.

This is me in a corner of our upstairs hallway that my mom reserved for me. I call it my "art gallery". It's where I go when I feel tired or down or overwhelmed. Turning on worship music and doing art here is the best. I love being able to keep my art supplies out all the time, and having my own space to be creative. Also, being able to hang my art on the wall makes me feel so happy. One time I even got to teach my dad how to do heart art that helped him express his feelings, right here in my art gallery. I love it!

This is me with my dad on my 8th birthday (about a year after I first wrote this book). Right after this picture was taken, the two of us went to The National Gallery of Art in Washington DC as a special birthday date! It was such a an awesome day. Getting to see some of the greatest paintings right in front of my eyes was the best!

This is my mom and me in Washington DC. Our church meets at that white tent just behind us on the National Mall. And earlier that day, I got baptised right there in the tent! The tent is called David's Tent - A prayer and worship ministry our friends started. We love going there to worship God with our friends and my favorite thing is to sit on the front row so I can be close to all the worship and teachings! I feel so happy there, because when I am at church, I feel God's presence.

This is me getting baptised on my 8th birthday- the same weekend
I got to go to the art museum with my dad! It was awesome! I felt
so sure that this was the weekend, my 8th birthday, that I wanted to
make a public statement of my love for Jesus- becuase of how much
He loves me! His love is my biggest encouragement.

This is Ms. Diane and me while we were in online tutoring one day. I like "in person" better, but with Covid-19, we are doing virtual. My mom took this so you could "meet" her, and know how awesome she is! Thank you, Ms. Diane, for helping me learn to overcome my challenges and for always being so nice!

Here I am with all of my brothers and sisters and mom and dad. We have a big family! But it is so much fun! This was an ice cream outing to celebrate my littlest brother's second birthday. Isn't he cute!?

I wrote this book when I was 7 and a half. But it took a while to get it published. This is me at my most recent birthday, turning 9. And now the book is finally published! I'm so happy that you have this book now, and hope that you can become more encouraged in your life, knowing you are not alone. You are loved!

Made in the USA
Las Vegas, NV
23 February 2021